Last Days of the Brooklyn Roundhouse and her Railway Steam Engines

For my Grandson Eli

Published in 2014 by Hvorfor Ikke, Walla Walla, Washington, USA. © Barbara Beito

Front cover photo by John Frazee, back cover by Barbara Beito

Library of Congress Control Number: 2015902190

All Rights Reserved

Available from Amazon.com and other retail outlets.

ISBN: 978 0 9886155 3 3

Last Days of the Brooklyn Roundhouse and her Railway Steam Engines

Barbara Beito
© 2013

The Brooklyn Roundhouse

The Brooklyn Rail Yard at 19th and S.E. Holgate Blvd. in Portland, Oregon has been in operation since around 1860. It was part of the Southern Pacific system prior to its merger with Union Pacific in 1997. The first Brooklyn Roundhouse, the northernmost end of the line for the Southern Pacific, was a 12 stall brick structure built in 1912 during the 2nd era railroad boom. Built to handle almost every class of repair the steam locomotives of the day might need, it was taken out of service in 1956 and razed in 1959. The roundhouse in this book, a 4 stall corrugated steel structure was built during the 1940s to accommodate the larger locomotives the previous roundhouse could not hold.

    A roundhouse wasn't necessarily round: as long as a turntable and tracks could be used to organize locomotives so inspection, cleaning, fueling, maintenance tasks and etc. could be centralized, the shelter could be round, square or in-between.

    At their peak, over 3,000 roundhouses were scattered through North America. By 2010 about 200 remained. Most of the old roundhouses were modernized and no longer serviced locomotives. The Brooklyn Roundhouse, the last intact Southern Pacific roundhouse, was one of approximately 67 still in railroad use.

    When the Southern Pacific – Union Pacific merged in 1997 Brooklyn's general freight yard became an intermodal yard. In 2012, after a 50 year injunction, agreements were reached that allowed the Union Pacific to modernize the Yard, reduce emissions and noise, and prepare the site for future re-development. Most of these pictures were taken during a visit to the Brooklyn

Yard in the spring of 2012 in an effort to make a record of a Pacific Northwest Roundhouse doing it's job: serving steam locomotives still in operation in an active train yard. The Brooklyn Roundhouse was torn down later that year to provide more area for the intermodal yard. The year of its destruction the Brooklyn Roundhouse had been the home of the SP&S 700 and the SP 4449, two giant Northern class steam locomotives. Both of these, and the OR&N #197 which was being rebuilt in the roundhouse, were moved to the new Oregon Rail Heritage Center which opened September 22nd of that year.

The Oregon Railroad and Navigation (OR&N) #197 was built in 1905 by Baldwin Locomotive Works as a 4-6-2 "Pacific" type locomotive. She weighs 200 tons, is 79' long with 77" drive wheels. Undergoing restoration at the time of these photos, she has a maximum track speed of 80 mph.

The Spokane Portland and Seattle (SP&S) #700, a 4-8-4 Northern Pacific Class A design built as an oil burner (E1 Class) was built in 1938 by Baldwin Locomotive Works in Philadelphia, Pennsylvania. She is almost 111' long by 17' tall. The open cab locomotive and tender weigh about 440 tons. With a boiler pressure of 260 psi and 77" drivers, she can exceed 80 mph and is rated at 5,000 horsepower.

The Southern Pacific (SP) #4449 was built as a 4-8-4 GS-4 "Daylight" locomotive in 1941 by the Lima Locomotive Works in Lima, Ohio. At 110' long and 16' tall, with a closed cab locomotive and tender weight of 433 tons, a boiler pressure of 300 psi, eight 80" diameter drivers and a turbine engine/booster for her trailing trucks, her 5,500 horsepower can drive down the rails at 100 mph and better. The #4449 pulled coaches for commercial passenger service for the Southern Pacific Railroad until retiring in 1955. She was restored in the 1970s, pulled the Bicentennial American Freedom Train in 1976 and continues to make occasional excursions.

Resources Consulted:

Culverwell, Wendy: **Portland Business Journal**, September 5, 2012.

Frazee, John: Oregon Rail Heritage Foundation Board of Directors 2010-2012. Personal Communication (Thank you, John).

Hankey, John: "The American Roundhouse" in **Trains** vol 70, no 3, March 2010, pages 24-33.

Oregon Rail Heritage Center, 2250 SE Water Avenue, Portland, OR

Oregon Rail Heritage Foundation, Newsletters and Press Releases, P O Box 42443, Portland, PR 97242

Norberg, Eric: "Union Pacific changes role of Brooklyn Train Yard" 9/30/09. **Brotherhood of Locomotive Engineers and Trainmen** press release.

1   Roundhouse (back) and crew office (front)

2	Old cab from the 197 (left) and new cab for the 197 (right)

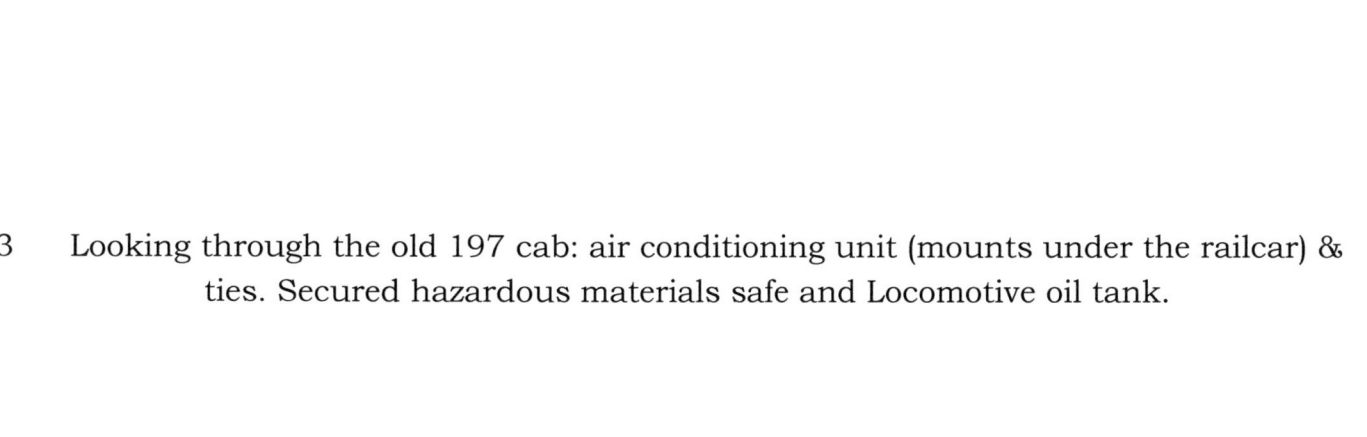

3   Looking through the old 197 cab: air conditioning unit (mounts under the railcar) & ties. Secured hazardous materials safe and Locomotive oil tank.

4   Side of the Roundhouse

5   Main Roundhouse doors and the SP 4449

6   Roundhouse: pedestrian entrance

7 Roundhouse: roof structure

8   Roundhouse side windows

9   OR&N 197 (without cab or tender) and skylight structure

10   OR&N 197 rods and drivers

11   OR&&N 197 (smoke box cover removed)

12   SP&S 700 front end

13   SP&S 700 builders numbers and below cab

14   SP&S 700 main drivers and side rods (note air pumps)

15   SP&S 700 main rods and drivers, alternate view

16	SP&S 700 Engineer's side

17   SP&S 700 Fireman's side control stand

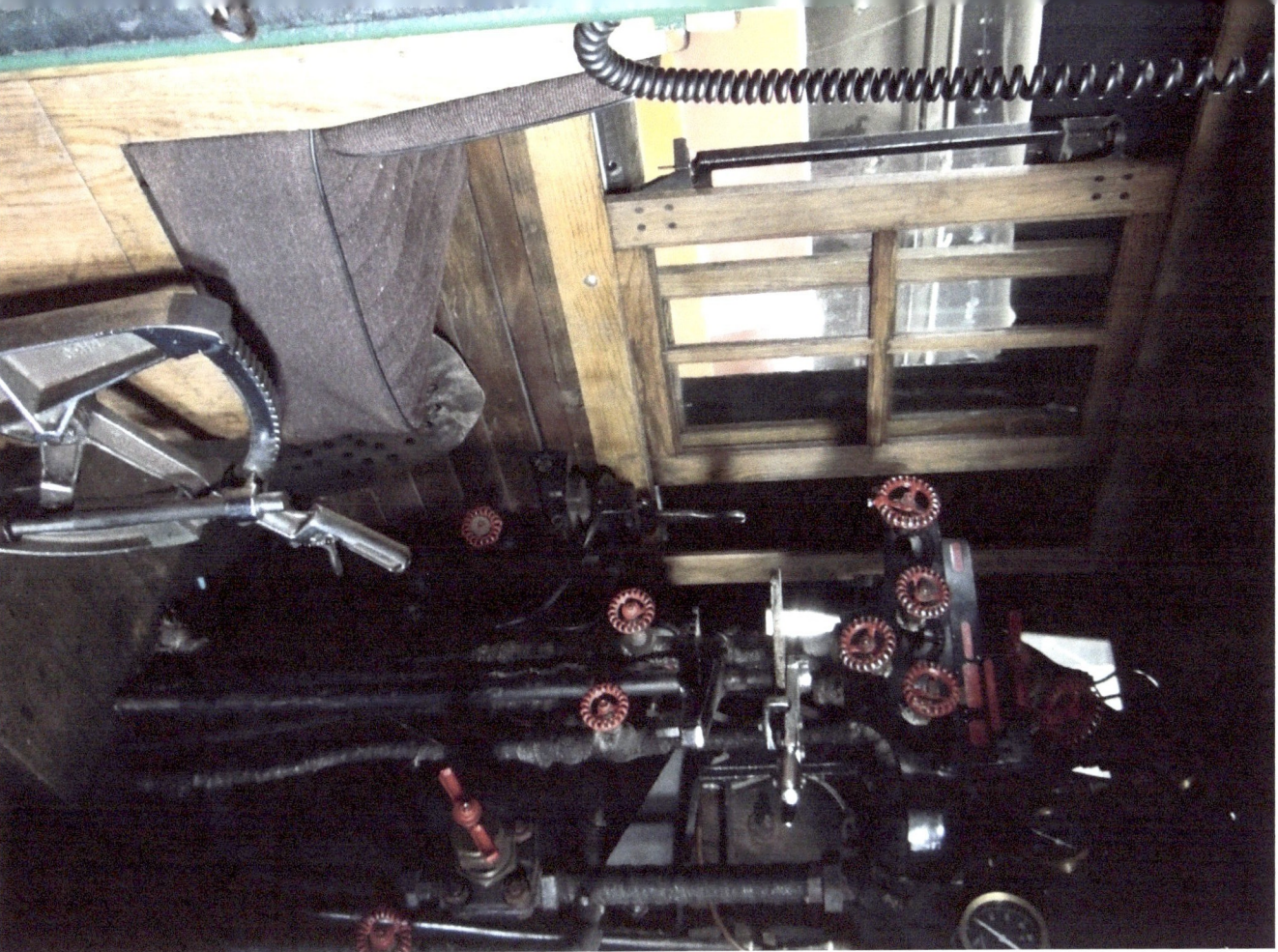

18   SP&S 700: fuel chart
(translates inches of fuel into gallons remaining)

19   SP 4449 front end
(note Mars lamp at top of smoke box cover)

20   SP 4449 Builder's numbers and Engineer's side

21   SP 4449 Controls

22   View from Roundhouse looking past turntable to container yard
(control cab on left)

23   Turntable pit

24 Roundhouse rear doors from turntable (note trackmobiles)

25   Last spin on the turntable: the OR&N 197 and the SP 4449

26   SP&S 700 underway: the Holiday Express

Barbara Beito now lives quietly in Washington State.

www.ingramcontent.com/pod-product-compliance
Lightning Source LLC
Chambersburg PA
CBHW041523090426
42737CB00037B/17